May God
the Father
Bless you

May God
the Son
Heal you

May God
the Holy Ghost
Enlighten you

Extinction
Copyri ght © 2018 by Tony Fusco
Cover Art, Book Design,
and Layout by Tony Fusco
ISBN #
978-0-9978562-5-5
All characters in this book are fictional.
Any resemblance to real persons living or dead
is purely coincidental.

This book is dedicated to my family, especially Patti, Emily, Cyndi, Stephen, Sean, Matthew, Alex, Nate, Wes and Dorothy.

A special thank you to Vivian Shipley and Pat Mottola for their advice and encouragement, and to all the poets who helped me workshop and refine some of these poems.

Extinction
poems by Tony Fusco

Table of Contents

Extinction

Before Coffee 11
The Twilight of America..13
That Kind of Woman..15
Wanna Be..17
I Want You 18
Flight Path..19
Identity Theft (Election 2016)....................................21
Extinction 24

Time Machine

Time Was 29
World Wars (in League with Nations).....................31
Parents of the Greatest Generation..........................32
Take Me...34
A Man Like Him 35
Un-Mentionables 38
It Was a Good Day to Stay in Bed 39
Again..40
Tin Type..41
POP 42
1969, Island Pond 44

Seven Deadly Sins

How Does That Make Me Feel (Anger) 49
Let's Get Going (Despair) 50
Self-Made Man 52
Don't Bother (Sloth) 53
When I Think About It (Envy) 55
Tax Cut (Greed) 57
Stalker (Lust) 58
A Second Opinion (Vanity) 59

Thinking Outside the Box

Thinking Outside the Box 63
Meet Me Again 64
The Last Dancing Witch 66
I Remembered the End of the World, Waking Last Night with a Fever 68
Beware the Dog 70
Apocalypse Rhymes 71
Start Without Me 73
The Long Shadows 75
Goodbye Forever 76

Extinction

Before Coffee

I might have missed the end of the world
last night which would go a long way to explain
why everything outside my house is gone.

It could be the reason the leaves are off
all the trees, the pine needles as well,
the evergreens green no more.

Maybe it is still a dark foggy night, or perhaps
the sun no longer shines, we just don't know
yet. Maybe there is no moon because

there is no moon. Shouldn't I have felt
a wobble or severe shaking at its fleeing,
its sneaking off into space, the dimensions

folding inside within themselves, the stars popping
out of their constellations, the skies now shapeless.
I should have expected a black hole

or inverted sphere sucking in all the cars,
the telephone poles, the beach blankets,
CNN News, the gangsters on the corner,

everything. Could I have slept through the screams
and all the other sounds of ripping and crashing,
politicians sucking wind, wind howling classical

and country music, Miley Cyrus on her
wrecking ball hitting the bricks on the way
out of the Galaxy? All my lost keys

and books and socks, the high school
yearbook, the Christmas card list
whooshed away in a blink. Just stuff

is what it is, or was. All I miss and wish
I had in my mug right now is sugar
and cream or some chariot swinging
sweet and low.

The Twilight of America

In the twilight of America
when all the lights went out
            there was no rapture
but there were bodies in the sky,
when prophets shed their sack cloth
            for designer suits and make-up,
when cities drowned,
        the wheat fields shriveled,
              the orchards dried up,
where books were barred,
          books were burned,
                books were left unread,
where no news was true news,
when the eyes of the people glazed over,
            the ears waxed full,
where dead diseases
                returned from the grave,
when the churches were closed,
           the pews already empty,
where armies killed enemies a world away
           without facing one another.
The earth shook
         the mud slid
              lightning filled the skies
like skeleton hands.
When the wind twisted
              its whirlwind, breaking great buildings,
when the towers fell
           when wild fires ate the landscape.

In the twilight of America
crowds fought in the parks
           with clubs and rocks and torches.
In the twilight of America
when everyone carried a rifle on a sling,
           a handgun in their handbags,

when children hid under desks in lockdown
                and runners blew to bits in the street.
In the twilight of America
the flag already hung at half mast
lowered itself the rest of the way down.

That Kind of Woman

A woman like her lets you think it was your idea,
writes her best lines at the bewitching hour,
inspires with charms.

A woman like her knows what she wants,
makes you glad you are a man.
Is not afraid, steps out on faith.

A woman like her would be a lover to wolves,
a mother to bears and owls and mice,
has kissed a lot of toads.

A woman like her is one who little black dresses
were made for, who struts her stuff,
who sways when she walks.

She's the kind of woman who respects your opinion.
The kind who inspects your opinion,
would rather be right, than proved right.

She's the kind of woman who flirts with her eyelashes,
has that come-hither look,
can look sexy in a witch's hat.

She's the kind of woman who has scarlet streaks
in her hair, who men beep their horns at,
who knows enough to walk away from a dead end.

She's the kind of woman who can talk you off the ledge,
gives dancing lessons at the senior center,
reads to blind veterans at the VA.

That kind of woman gets up at 4 a.m. to paint watercolors
before the kids wake up, then
drives the kids to school in her pajamas.

She leaves milk out for the neighborhood cat,
bakes cookies with neighborhood children, is someone
people talk about behind her back because she's just a mom
and doesn't work.

That kind of woman takes the kids to church on Sunday
while her husband sleeps, takes the kids for a ride
when the game is on.

That kind of woman is strong as iron, as malleable
as mashed potatoes; she does not need nor has ever read
a cookbook. She knows what side her bread is buttered on.

A woman like her longs to be held in strong arms,
has never been to Paris. Only cries when she is alone
in the bathroom.

A woman like her has a hairdresser who knows
nothing about her real life. A woman like her
has a tattoo lurking somewhere below her navel.

A woman like her drinks white wine in the restaurant,
Jack Daniels at the bar. She doesn't need to have you
explain the dirty joke.

A woman like her never wears lipstick
when she is out with a married man,
has never been in the back seat of a car.

A woman like her dances on the summer lawn
in the moonlight. A woman like her doesn't give a damn
what you think of a woman like her.

Wanna Be
(after Christine Beck's "Civil Action")

I want to be your romance,
your leopard pants,
partner of your last dance.
I want to be your stockings fine,
your rescue line.
I want to be your nights in France.

I want to be your cloud nine,
your one way sign,
your both rain or shine.
I want to be your bedtime muse,
your dynamite-igniting fuse,
I want to be your intertwine.

I want to be your spike-heel shoes,
your morning news,
your exotic island cruise.
I want to be your cause for joy,
your western saddle hard-cowboy.
I want to be your rose tattoos.

I want to be your favorite toy,
Paris to my Helen of Troy,
your cabin boy.
I want to be your mattress cover,
your dreamboat rudder,
your heartbeat flutter.
I want to be your delivery boy.

I want to be your soft churned butter,
your last supper, the last name you utter.
I want to be your heart's desire,
your deepest spot ablaze with fire.
I want to be your poetry lover.

I Want You

I want you like the ocean wants back
every grain of sand from the shore.

I want you like a repeating mantra,
a skipping record, three knocks on the door.

I want you the way water wants
to find its own level,
the way it bubbles up in the mud hole
refilling the endless beach bucket.

I want you like gravity pulls
at everything in its reach,
the way time bends
in your presence.

I want you the way a monk longs for silence
and fire for the dry fall grass,
like wind for the last hidden nook,
dust for the empty book shelf.

I want you like quicksand
wants to hug you forever,
like the magnet seeks its opposite,
like a North pole wants the South.

I want you like the fish cannot
let go the hook,

like I am trapped in the web.
I want you like the very first-time.

I want you like the poem
wants to find its ear.

Flight Path

Save me a seat in the car in your garage.
I'm on my way.
I'm coming like Judgment Day,
I'm coming like the last asteroid,
I'm coming like the end of time's little black pill,
I'm coming like ISIS riding a Toyota
into drone central.
I'll be there like the 2nd amendment.
I'll be there like inheritance taxes,
I'll be there like probate court,
like Title Nineteen.
I'll be there like stockbrokers on a Monday,
like the White House Press,
like the Supreme court press.
I will elect to depart
from the election trail.
Save me some space in the deepest of coal mines,
the failing coral reef, the sink holes,
the hollow mountains.
Save me the edge on the melting ice floe,
the shrinking poles, the polar bear dining club.
I'll be back at the reservation before closing time.
I'll be gone before last call at Mory's.
There's no need to wait for me,
but it would be nice.
I'll be coming the way of all flesh,
coming on a day in ordinary time,
coming before the black bird sings.
I'll be coming before the bird flu,
the swine flu, the mosquito pandemic.
I'm in the race to end the race.
I won't get caught in the human trafficking.
I'm paying attention to the stop signs,
the off ramp, the no-you return signs,
the internal combustion engine,
frontal lobe dementia,

brain plaques and tangles,
MS and degenerative cancer.
I'll be limping my way through
Pharmacology and the twelve steps
of self-abuse. I am long on living
and short on housing,
short on time,
short of compassion.
I am done with the travelogue,
done with desire.
I can't wait till next season.
I won't need a stone,
my last marker was called in.
I'll deal with the cold,
I'll deal with the devil
if he has the balls to show up.
I'm coming with you, or alone.
You need not leave the door open.
I'll be coming rest assured,
and assuredly most of all
not along for the ride.

Identity Theft (Election 2016)

I won't be showing up for the next big thing.
I won't be standing in line to vote
for the lesser of three evils.
I will not need to bring my ID

and passport to prove I am white enough
or how many shades of dark Italians hide
in my family woodpile.

I won't be standing in line in the village
square for my fair share of guns and butter,
my senior citizen cheese.

I won't be waiting for my number to come up,
my lottery winner, the door-crack draft,
nor volunteering my selective services.

I won't be waiting in the parking lot
on Black Friday for the latest bargain
of a lifetime, quantities limited.

I won't be shoving dollar bills
into the G-strings of pole dancers
or quarters into slot machines.

I won't be standing in line at the all-
you-can-eat Native American buffet,
or fracking South Dakota, or fracking
the check-out girl at Stop and Shop
or toeing the line at the serve-yourself
no-union cash registers.

I won't be encouraging the 50 shades of grey
or reading between the stripes of the 50 red,
and white states, white for

the fundamentalists, black for the ones
owned by the coal and oil companies.

I won't be exchanging my social security
for stocks and bonds, for derivatives,
for low interest low-brow loans.

I will not give up on the soul of America
the one before the assassination of JFK,
the Moon shot,
the murder of Martin Luther,
the death of intellect, the climate change
on college campuses. The freedom
bell curve of Patriotism and of Justice.

I will not stand in line with my *Hands Up*.
Be caught again with my pants down.

I will no longer wear the suspenders of disbelief
or tolerate a Stars and Bars flag of heritage.

The *Ode to the Confederate Dead* is dead.
The Brain Trust is the only trust
that I will ever put my trust or future in,
and one of The Bill of Rights the only Right
I will ever believe again.

I won't stand on circumstances
but make the politicians stand
on their vinyl record collections,
not allow them to get away
with just scratching the surface
of the fundamental Rights to Life.

I won't be showing up for the Rapture.
I'll make sure I'm not found or drafted
or end-listed. I plan to disappear

deep into the heart-less land long before that
 America, un-friend me if you must.

Extinction

The people cried out
the poor in their lean-to's
the homeless in cardboard boxes
those sleeping on rooftops in the desert night
those sleeping on satin sheets in studio apartments
the people in brick and wood and straw houses
people in glass houses, people in tents,
children in shacks and marble halls,
seniors in hospitals
couples in trailer parks
couples in casinos
couples in the soup kitchens
cried out. People in revolving doors,
people in house boats,
refugees in inflatable rafts
people in the underground cities,
small towns, villages, retirement condos.
The inmates cried out
the dog pounds of lost souls,
they all cried out.

The animals cried out.
The beached whales cried out,
the crated chickens cried out,
the life blood of steers and cows
of oxen, of pigs, of lambs,
the livers, the gizzards, the kidneys
of fowl, and bears cried out.
Everything that eats and grows
wailed to the high heavens.

Statues and famous paintings
cried out from museums
and it fell on stone ears.
Strung instruments vibrated
with their complaints,

monuments would not remain silent,
books burned
in their desire to speak, to be understood.

The hills and the mountains cried out.
The wandering winds cried out,
the hail and rain cried out,
the flash floods, the rising tides,
the sandstorms,
the sea cliff's jagged edges,
the broken boulders,
the twisted wheat and wild grasses,
the muddy oily rivers, the tire-filled streams
the piped and enclosed brooks
and catch basins,
the shrinking ice shelves,
the thawing tundra,
the warming oceans,
the dying kelp,
the aquatic food chain,
the hardening and sulfurous lava vents,
the cradles and the boiling birthing
pyres of life cried out.

They all cried out.
They all cried for Justice,
until God threw a great stone at the world.

Time Machine

Time Was

Time was the shortest distance between
two points was a bicycle.

Time was you and your friends would drink
from a garden hose.
Time was everyone had a nick-name
not a password.

Time was shoes only came in two colors
and the store only carried one.
Time was snow and hill and saucer
was a wild ride

Time was home grown meant
a tomato from your vegetable garden.
Time was when the lights went out,
out came the candles and board games.

Time was someone was a rich man
if he owned a dog.
Time was when soap floated
when clothes dried on a rope,

when one had to leave the house
to go to the bathroom,

when three shared a bed.
Time was when everything was
new and improved.

Time was when it didn't matter if your pants
had a patch on the knee.
Time was when you *wanted* to read
the small print and could.

Time was only the bad guys wore black hats
and you could tell them apart.

Time was when a minute of her time
was the only time you wanted.

Time was when scary was only
what was in the dark corner of your basement.

Time was when the only gun in school
was a staple gun.

Time was when your doctor always had the answer.

Time was when time was the only thing
you always thought you would have enough of.

World Wars (in League with Nations)

It began in alliances and ended in mayhem.
It began on horseback and ended in tanks,
began with torpedoes and ended with wolf packs,
began with a Czar and ended with a monster,
began with a Kaiser and ended in *the Reichstag* burning.

It began in open fields and farmland
and ended in a cratered grave.

It began in trenches and grew wings,
began with gallantry and ended in killing efficiency,
began with U-boats and ended in dark cold depths.

It began with volunteers and ended with a draft.

It began with bullets and ended in mustard gas,
began with medical advances, ended in the flu epidemic,
began with flamethrowers and ended in hell,
was born in the mass production of bombs,
of ships, machine guns, barbed wire.

It grew up to end the old world
with one assassination.

It began in national pride
with flags, with parades,
with speeches and church picnics,
began with wide smiling youth,
and ended in mass murder.

Parents of the Greatest Generation

Theirs were the years of petticoats and outhouses.
The turn of one hundred years, of precious metals
dug and blasted out of the ground and pressed
into coins and fine chains of pocket watches.

Theirs the years of waxed mustaches and sock garters,
of gramophone cylinders and gas lights,
electric lines and breadlines, trolley lines,
of sideshow x-rays and moving pictures,
Typhoid Mary, the yellow fever.

Theirs were the years of the birth of flight,
the tommy gun, speakeasy jazz,
and gangsters, *America First* and the *Daughters
of the American Revolution*, the sisterhood

of temperance and suffrage, the age of news
print and a nation of isolation dragged
into the trenches of a war to end all wars,
the war that emptied the farmyards and filled
pockets of profiteers and arms merchants.

Theirs were the years of immigrant slums,
of Sacco and Vanzetti,
of loyalty tests, of Uncle Sam
and Lady Liberty hand in hand,
selling bonds and building ships,
Remington, Marlins, Winchesters
and Colts, carbines and cartridges,
years of light bulbs, sewing machines,
typewriters and washing machines,
refrigerators and long-distance calls.

Theirs were the years of prohibition,
the Legion of Decency, the depression
that followed, theirs the hard winters,

the home grown vegetables,
the Americanization
of their children,
the dreams of the working class.

Take Me

Take me like a mother reaches for her newborn.

Take me like an unexpected kiss.

Take me like you would a melting gelato on a hot July night.

Take me like the downhill rush of a landslide.

Embrace me like you have been waiting four billion years.

Embrace me like you forgot who we were.

Embrace me like it was your last day alive.

Consume me like wild fire does the drought forest.

Do it like a thief who comes back again and again.

Steal it like the dancing flame the soul.

Trust me like a waterfall takes the plunge
sliding soft and easy over smooth river stone.

Take me like the lovers in the field,
like the buttercup glow on smiling chins.

Take me like the bear does honey,
lick-lickery-ing the sweet sticky fur.

Draw me in like a white table cloth
sucks in the spilled wine.

Take me like it's the very first time.

A Man Like Him

A man like him buys you a card the day
of your anniversary
on his way home from work.

A man like him loves to cook and bake
but doesn't do dishes or pans.

A man like him has more tools than he'll ever need
but not the one to stop the leaky sink.

He's the kind of man who can put his feet up
and have a beer.

He's the kind who asks
what program you would like to watch,
but will never hand you the remote.

When he could do almost anything,
he chooses to blow bubbles with the kids.

He's a guy who never looks at his watch,
a guy who cries at Betty Davis movies.

He will never eat yogurt unless it is mistaken
for ice cream.

He's the kind of man who reads
Camus and Sartre but cannot pronounce
the names correctly.

A man like him goes to Mass on Sundays
and confession on Monday night.

A man like him can unstick a window and fix
a boo boo with the same fingers.

He thinks beef jerky is an appetizer,
pork rinds an entree.

He orders Cabernet on your first date,
brings a six pack of Duff beer to the next.

A man like him inspires you
to move mountains,
who finds adventure in his own back yard.

A man like him takes "no" for an answer.

He's the kind of man who looks good in a muscle tee shirt,
whose kisses taste like apple pie.

He is the kind of man who drives a 14-year-old Volvo.
A guy who doesn't think board games are for children.

This man has a tattoo on his right arm that says "Mom"
and one on the other that says "Nietzsche Is Dead."

He has a shoulder you can cry on.
His marker plate says "Born to Raise Children."

He washes the car in the rain to save water.
A guy like him always knows a short cut,
plays classical music on his iPod,
pulls the weeds like an avenging angel.

He is a guy who works out
at the gym then goes out
for some fried chicken wings
with the guys,

a guy who leaves the strawberry for you
in the Neapolitan ice cream,
the cherry on the top of a sundae.

He's the kind of man who makes you look twice
and melt thrice.

A man like him crowd-sources his poetry.

Un-Mentionables

Under the long skirts
the pilgrim collars
the burka and hijab
the laced and constrained
whale stays of corsets
under the bed
the buttoned undergarment
the bloomers, the knickers
the zippered jeans
the waist huggers
and pedal pushers
the hook laced brassiere
the knee highs
the thigh high boots
the hoop skirts
beneath the bustles
and booster bodice
the multilayer teddies
and camisoles
the tank tops
the halter tops
the wrap around
the underskirt
under the petticoats
the slip
the half slip
the slip of the tongue
hide the parts that are Woman.

It Was a Good Day to Stay in Bed

It was the day of the dead.
It was the day after the day before yesterday
when the jailer consulted the Egyptian
Book of the Dead, the *Necronomicon* missing
the important pages concerning reanimation.

It was just what was left behind
in the rush of the revelation,
that the Rapture was canceled without
further notice, no rain date, just the storm
preceding the run on survivalist equipment,
the half-price sale and guarantee of innumerable
targets, hard tack and powdered milk.
It was a retailer's week of Black Fridays.

It was this crazy big group of daemons and ghouls,
cannibals and pirates, and conflicted superheroes.
It was as if every holiday was Halloween
for real and every month was a month of holidays
and everyone was forced to observe them.

It was the sun disappearing from the sky,
the moon crashing into the sea, the spinning
wheel of Andromeda and the spilled
milk of the Milky Way all over
everyone's Sunday best go-to-church wardrobe.

It was *King Crimson's* blood-red clock
that read the odd numbers only.
It was the witching hour that came twice a day
as it was the best of the worst of time.

Again

If I let her leave today,
She would take her songs and go.
Hasn't that always been my way?

I gave in too easily one could say.
I should have tried harder I know.
If I let her leave today,

If I let her just slip away,
I could lie, not let my feelings show.
Hasn't that always been my way?

Tired in thoughts and drowsy I stray,
As the remaining embers lose their glow.
If I let her leave today,

Portents unravel, tomorrows fray,
Risking all on one fortune's throw.
Hasn't that always been my way?

To choose loneliness at the end of the day,
Ignore the heart that screams no, no,
When I let her leave today.
Hasn't that always been my way?

Tin Type

Stiff and hardened into metal
a sculpture in light and acid,
take this one into battle
in your breast pocket,
close to your heart.

Take your brother stood up on end
in his small casket, one last look
for a family with six children,
only three surviving to adulthood.

Put it on the mantel shelf,
in a cigar box, dresser drawer.

Preserve a shadow house in the background
a gray tinted barn, immortal horses
caught frozen head over the fence
forever, so near a held apple,
wrangler holding a bridle,
hens and chicks of ten generations ago.

Colors, flesh, warmth, the sweet scent
of zinnias, the magnesium lingering
of studio flash powder fume
dissipates on the breeze,
developing over the flattened
cold likeness,
embedded for eternity.

POP

He didn't need a license to drive
just needed to know how to steer and to work
a clutch, and to borrow a vehicle.

Outside the city, after work and on Sundays
the bubble-tired pickup truck bounced
over unpaved roads, across the railroad tracks
out to the *farm*--how they did it in the old country.

Not his land technically, cultivated tended and
watered for a bartered share of the yield
from an older couple too far along Americanization
to be working with their hands in the dirt.

Such great loam, black earth virtually untouched
for thousands of years. Everything grows there
everything thrives, squash, eggplant, tomatoes,
cucumbers, corn, even with such short growing

seasons. More than enough for the family,
enough to sell or trade on the hot summer
door stoops and stairs, to can and preserve

in boiled glass jars, store in a cool basement
and cellar for winter. Grandchildren enough
to fill and carry bushels, baskets, tools, buckets,

each going with Pop until old enough
to find paying work, making way
for the next oldest to replace them.

They would still need the whole crew
to pick the strawberries and blackberries,
to crush the grapes--and later,

in reused glass Gallo bottles,
deliver and share
the finished gallons of wine.

1969, Island Pond

It was the summer of *Canned Heat* and *Light My Fire*
blared on the 8-track player of the overheated Chevy Biscayne,
V-6 pumping away up Interstate 91 arriving at dawn.

It was the summer of *Lay Lady Lay, Strawberry Fields,*
cowboy hats, beards and hand-carved walking sticks,
Smirnoff straight from the bottle in hidden cornfields.

It was the summer of the *Weight* having just *Pulled
into Nazareth* and *One Toke Over the Line*
in a smoke filled hunting lodge in Vermont.

It was summer nights of the *Moody Blues,
Knights in White Satin, Days of Future Past,*
of youth hostel bikers, forty-seven teenage girls
and six twenty-year-old chaperones.

It was the night of drinks at the *Buck N Doe* bar,
the cocktail smorgasbord, the VFW hall
with the village drunk, Vice President Agnew's

picture over the door, the night of Scott falling
off his ten speed, a broken collar bone,
twelve black Russians, feeling no pain.

It was the night of screaming folk songs
atop the M4 Sherman tank on the green, *Country Joe
and the Fish, The Fish Cheer, What are we fighting for?*

It was the strange things making funny moves
in the star-packed sky. *Please Mr. Spaceman
won't you please take me along for the ride?*

It was the swirling points of light approaching,
crisscrossing over the open field, forty-seven
bike lights in pursuit of David's pickup.

It was Sherri the mousy twenty-one-year-old
doubled over in the corner, who next morning
needed a lift to the nearest hospital, needed dialysis.

It was the morning of Scott's X-ray broken collarbone,
the revealing of Sherri's death sentence; waiting
the morning for her parents to come drive her home,
and an afternoon, evening and tomorrow totally wasted.

Seven Deadly Sins

How Does That Make Me Feel (Anger)

I am bringing the whirlwind
upon your head, sharpening my knives,
carrying a baseball bat in the back seat,
recording your movements,
nibbling at the edges of your life,
searching for a soft spot,
mailing you rose-less thorns,
spray painting your house
with obscene graffiti,
driving away your friends and neighbors,
isolating your relatives.
I will hurt you through them.

I will cost you your job,
slice the lining of your swimming pool
before kicking in your tail lights,
smashing your windshield,
cutting your brake lines,
turning you black and blue,

all this before stealing your identity,
hacking your Tinder account,
poisoning your cat,
kidnapping your Chihuahua,
drowning your hamster,
burning your furniture,
tapping into your bank account,
spiking your tea with LSD,
splashing you with blood.

I have plans for piercing your body,
ripping off your clothes,
dismembering your members,
selling your body parts.
I can't wait to see you there sweetheart,
where we can discuss it in Hell.

Let's Get Going (Despair)

Come on, the bus is waiting.
The candle's burning down,
burning on both ends.

Come on, we will miss the beginning;
there will be no coming attractions.

There's already a crowd.
We can get there first or last,
the ticket puncher won't care.

The ice cream is melting
and you can see the laughing
fat lady in the window,
hear the old *Wild Mouse*,
his *Laff in the Dark*,
the false alarm
blaring like an air raid.

Hurry, Mom's on the lawn
and the grass is on fire!

Hurry! There is only so much time
in Eternity for us two. Get along
little doggies, the sun dial says
it's later than what you see
on the face of it.

Get going, you have to grow up.
Believe me children, there's nothing
to contemplate,
no short cuts.

The escalator
is too slow, the elevator too high

and uplifting. The sour bread is rising;
the south is rising again and again.

The wise guys are back and in the catacombs.

Come on, don't fiddle about your make up.

Don't make up tales. Who has the patience
to hear them? The locomotive
has jumped the rails.

Come on now,
don't get all weepy,
don't cut out the newspaper pieces,
don't laminate and pushpin
the memorial photos.

This town's crumbling like Jericho
at one horn's blast.

The countdown has stalled
at the square root of one.

The pendulum is hung up
on the grandfather clock.

Come on, that final paper is due.
There's one in the chamber,
but no one's there waiting for you.

Self-Made Man

> *Who are you going to believe, me or your own eyes?*
> --Julius Henry Marx

I am who I say I am,
the real deal, the real McCoy.
I write my own story.
No point in seeking authenticity
questioning or probing further for insight.

Nothing in my past could prove the point,
explain an empire from kindergarten building blocks,
or fourth grade drawings of ink-spotted
monsters and large breasted women on book covers,
or military school discipline;
not the guiding hand and lessons
of a wealthy father could reveal
how I have done it all myself.

The past is all those lost childhood wishes on a star,
the pennies down the well, the three coins
into the fountain, a wave of ripples
grown longer and flatter by distance.
I can only tell you I am more than
a collection of everything I have encountered.
I tell you honestly I am the real thing,
as true and solid, better.

Not my parents' desires, not Fate or Destiny's pawn.
People always choose me
with no other help provided or asked for,
I do what I want to, when I want to.
I owe no one. Even ask the liars,
they will tell you God gave me free will,
because I would have taken it anyway.

Don't Bother (Sloth)

It is the Eleventh Hour,
slugs and snails cross the floor.
The grasshopper plays his fiddle.

He is only half asleep,
goofing off on a weekday, nothing
to do, nothing better to do, nothing
he cares to do.

The phone rings,
he doesn't answer. It might be
something important, most likely not.

Snack wrappers and crumbs surround
his cushioned den,
his blanket-shrouded man cave.

He could eat more, but that would
entail getting up and finding something,
going to the store, or asking someone else.

Colleagues nick-named
him *slacker. Name calling
is so non-productive*, he shrugs.

He is currently unemployed,
unemployable. He'll check the want ads
when he gathers up the steam,
opens the door, ambles to the end
of the driveway to pick up the paper.
Bruegel's painting *Desidia* is in the
inside of the arts section.

There's pain in his melancholy litany,
complaints of bad back, bad legs
bad timing. One day, he says

he will take a shower. No, better
yet a bath. What to do when
the water becomes cold? Not so
good an idea.

On his tablet
Candy Crush, Farm Land, Tiny Towers,
games unfinished.

He might argue
these indictments with you,
that is, if it wasn't too much of a trouble.

When I Think About It (Envy)

I
I am jealous for a hundred-foot yacht
in Boston Harbor,
I am jealous of the rich,
jealous of tall men,
jealous of men whose clothes fit right,
men who eat and don't gain waist size,
jealous of the tenors,
the smooth voices, the microphone voices,
jealous of those who play a musical instrument.

I am jealous of those born before me,
enjoyed the benefits of low mortgages
and high interest. Those being
in the right place at the right time.
I am jealous of the young,
especially the young, as there are daily
so many more of them.
I am jealous of the confident,
the self-assured, the dream weavers,
the silver tongued.

II
I envy the guys who grew up
in your neighborhood, who went to your school,
sat next to your desk. Jealous of the guys
who called you, who met you at the beach.

I am angry with the guys you had a crush on,
the guys who dumped you,
cheated on you, took you for granted,
the guys who ruined you for romance,
the stalkers, guys who made you weary of men,
women who pretended to be your friend,

angry with bigoted mothers, possessive fathers,
brothers, gossip mongers, heart thieves,
the guy who caught you by surprise and kissed you.

I am jealous I am not the one with you now.
I am jealous of the unwrinkled,
the non-balding, the spotless,
the headache free,
the backache free,
the cramps and tingling free,
the footloose and fancy free.
I am jealous for all to see.

Tax Cut (Greed)

It is never enough, be it beads
or sea shells, bits of glass
or animal hides, a slave's sweat
and striving.

As the pyramid grows taller,
the base must grow wider,
bearing the crushing weight of stone.

Coins with holes in them,
barrels of oil, tusks of ivory,
promises and pledges,
obligations, papers with numbers,

documents of ownership, measure
how thick a stack a single life is worth,
how many lives controlled, crushed
together and banded.

What little you have
is a little too much,
but for the kings,
the captains of industry,

the back room boys,
the bosses, the collectors,
the counters,
it is always just a start.

Stalker (Lust)

I caress her body from across the room.
No longer myself, my drive is on auto pilot.
It is biological, it is *pheromones*, it doesn't matter.
Her sexual attraction entangles me.
My senses are alert, body language changes.

Does she realize or no, the force that pulls
at me, the magnetic attraction. It doesn't matter
if it is the way she walks, the sway, the jiggle,
the framed face and smile, something in her
glance that speaks without words. I listen,
I wait.

I don't want to be her friend,
the bloodhound is on her trail. Chance
has nothing to do with it. I manipulate
for us to be together. I have imagined her
touch, her taste, her shape and skin
beneath her clothing. In a fog, I am focused,
view her only as through a tunnel.

She has ceased to be a person to me.
She is not a girl, a mother, someone's
sister or wife. She is a goal,
one I rush to like a river's raging rapids.

Does no one else feel the heat,
are they lost in the false theater,
the false reality, do they play at being
civilized? I am animal. No obstacles,
no bend of path, no restraint.
I must have her.
I hunger for her,
and have her or not
I am starving.
I am wasting away.

A Second Opinion (Vanity)

You seem very intelligent,
impartial, able to balance and discern.
Tell me truly what you see, hold nothing back.

Right, of course no one is perfect.
I would expect a flaw or two, a freckle
here, blotch there: that goes without saying,
but tell me overall, your impressions,
reflect on how I fit in with the rest?

Way above average I already know.
Am I not a sight? Yes a bad angle
can always be found. How's this one? No,
this I am sure is the worst. I never liked

myself in profile. Okay, I will admit
the hair is thinner, but it is silver
not gray. Yes, it is inconsistent
across my body, shades of my old
brown color fading, darker in other
spots. I'm not eighteen anymore.

Oh that hurts. You knew me at eighteen?
Ideas of beautiful and handsome change
over time. There are different rubrics today.

I have a noble nose. What? I mean
it's a Roman nose, broken in football--
that adds character. Plenty of people say

I'm looking good. The weight is acceptable
for this age. *Well, who asked you?*

Oh right! Well who are you to judge?
Leave it to you to get things backwards,

everything is turned around for you
isn't it? I'm getting dressed, you know
the clothes make the man. Listen to me,

that's quite enough, those things
are designed for skinny mannequins;
only freaks fit well with off-the-rack
stuff. I am a normal size, most people
are short. Most people have necks

larger than the shirt sizes. You and I are done!
I'm sorry I looked to you to begin with.
A little glass and silver paint, your kind

are a dime a dozen, mass produced
in China. I prefer an artist's interpretation.
Damn right I'm an artist!

The mirror shatters as the fist in a ball
crashes. Seven years of bad luck.
It is well worth it, you ingrate.

Thinking Outside
the Box

Thinking Outside the Box

Try to forget about it,
but don't forget too much.

Put your thoughts in a happy place
and tether them as best you can.

Pick and change your clothes,
your lovers,
your dinners and desserts.

Check off the list the piddling stuff,
the big projects with deadlines.
Deadlines never end; they stretch
into the sunset, where
vacations and diversions are consumed.

Surprises are just
that, when you are not expecting
the knock, the bell to ring.

Even the most dependable watch
is of no use.

Time does not exist,
except on this side of Paradise.

Meet Me Again

Meet me the last place we met
if you can remember standing
in the street, an awkward then un-releasing
hug. My saying I'll never see you again,
you answering I couldn't know that
with certainty.

Meet me at the train station platform
and the fog frosted windows,
seeing you first and studying your
face's plain expression blooming
into a smile when you catch sight of me
running to keep up with the moving
doorway.

Meet me on your bedroom floor
babysitting your brother, record
playing Peter, Paul and Mary,
Where have all the flowers gone?
Folk songs and holding hands.

Meet me in the Friday night hayfield,
half-empty bottle of gin, jelly jar glasses
on the dash of an overheated Chevy
Impala laughing at the rutting
of friends in the backseat.

Meet me on your parents' doorstep
three in the morning, everyone asleep
trying to gift me a birthday presence
I fail even to acknowledge,
rushing off to be kept awake all night
staring at the dark, figuring it out.

Meet me on the seawall
under a midsummer moon of madness,

empty bottle of wine, huddled against
a cold last-chance breeze
blowing through the rocks.

Meet me forty-seven years ago
finely dressed, suited, pressed shirt,
late as usual, in church, arm in arm
down the aisle walking into the far
far future as if it were this morning.

The Last Dancing Witch

The magic has dried up like dead heads
of garden-patch herbs and flowers,
roses hung upside down, sachets that have lost
their fragrance. Just a few peaceful years before,
with her sisters skyclad in the illumination
of the full moon, she gathered mushrooms
from fallen tree limbs from fairy circles where
lightning had cleared bramble stages.

They are gone, and there were others, vital,
alive, reaching for heaven flying ergot anointed,
seducing ointment massaged into pores,
into the darkest most secret of places,
a small imitation of *St. Vitus's Dance*,
the entire village spellbound
in the thrall of *St. Anthony's Fire* wild,

ripping off clothing, lunging and spinning,
rolling in the mud, orgasmic to a rhythm
to a shared music, convulsing, inhibitions
gone, farmers and traders, nobles and vagrants,
clerics and convent freed in a frenzy
of movement and sensation.
Curse the black death that has taken all,
that evil, that unforgiving, that lord of equality,
skeleton monster, grinning skull.

All the huts, the cities, the great halls and courts,
markets and shipyards, empty.
Survivors hermited away, walled in and cautious,
hunt even the bare whisper of the sacred reel,
stalk with ropes and fire, torture and fervor.

The charm of spiders' bites is gone.
The flooded rye fields un-kept give way
to wheat and corn, cultivation.

The secret lore of the ancients, the ritual
stages of initiation dissipate,

age-erasing memories
gnawing at them like rats in the grain barn,
lost for centuries the time of innocence,
of pleasure, carnal fulfillment, yielding
to the natural, that animal enchantment
going the way of flesh,

the hair, the skin and the sweat
buried unmarked on hillsides and crossroads,
burned and spread in fields from buckets of ash
or left hung to feast the blackbirds
and the flying ballet of flies.

I Remembered the End of the World, Waking Last Night with a Fever

The air raid whistle blew every night at six p.m.,
hangover from World War Two, civil defense,
the cold war, ever since the Russians
stole the secrets to the H-bomb, since
the Rosenbergs sold out America,
since Khrushchev shouted he would bury us.

The siren became routine, many marking
time never wondering how the tradition
came to be. Missiles in Cuba filled Saint Paul's
church confessionals. Our family prayed
with rosary beads on Friday evenings,
with a candle and the smell of fish

lingering in the air. I dreamt
it was after dark and late for home,
when the screaming of the alert came

different this time, not ending after a few
blasts, but blaring, Gabriel's trumpet,
Heimdall's *Gjallarhorn, the drone of doom.*

My house on the hill lit up and the doors
open, waiting for me. I was not afraid to die,
wanted to be with them, know we were together

safe or not, just not alone. Radiation
drifted down like giant red snowflakes
sticking to everything, death lint on the sky,

the road, the cornfield. I had to jump
the brook, race through
the dry corn stalks, careless of what

they might shelter in my desire
to be with my mom and dad, my sister,
to hug them and wait together

for the siren's all clear we knew
this time would not be coming,
but would wail on forever over
our irradiated neighborhood
clinging to the scarlet backdrop
as we endured our diminishing half-lives.

Beware the Dog

The black dog
that hateful thing
swooning shadow
bogey beast,
paws the night's
dark recesses
burning crimson eyes
exposing canines
yellow as dirty moonlight.
Padfoot, Churchyard Beast,
Hell Hound, the devil's mongrel
between the wooded wall
like tall temple columns
an omen, a predator.
Unwelcome news.
Its wolf-like snarls
drool as it sniffs at old hands,
arthritic fingers that clutch
the three o'clock bed covers.

Apocalypse Rhymes

It is the end of the world,
when it snows in July.

It is the end of the world,
when the pigs start to fly.

It is the end of the world,
when old crocodiles cry.
The world will end,
this next hour.

It is the end of the world,
in some meteor showers.

It is the end of the world,
when wild fire devours.

It is the end of the world,
where a new religion flowers.
The world will end,
when we are still sleeping.

It is the end of the world,
when the stockbrokers are weeping.

It is the end of the world,
when it was all in our keeping.

It is the end of the world,
with the grim reaper reaping.
This world will end,
and our friends finally matter.

It is the end of the world,
when the mountains become flatter.

It is the end of the world,
while the talking heads chatter.

It is the end of the world,
as the debt collectors gather.
The world will end,
to sad faces and bright smiles.

It is the end of the world,
with ardent denials.

It is the end of world,
no juries, no trials.

The world will end,
as her last horseman passes
leaving no one to clean up
the horseshit.

Start Without Me

You would be late for your own funeral.
It sounds like a good plan to me.
My grandmother's admonishment rarely aimed
in my direction as I am punctual to a fault,
most likely to arrive early
and have to wait in the ER hallway,
or maybe set the alarm clock to wail
just before I might fail to wake up one night;
timing is everything after all.

Really, wouldn't it be prudent to arrive beyond
the appointed hour for whatever good reason
or fault you could come up with, such as
not having the right thing to wear to such
a big event? There being no sense to it
not to spiff up, or shave, maybe even run
a comb through the thinning hair.

I might blame construction on the interstate,
traffic causing a pain in the ass today,
two lanes closed with flares,
flashing lights, rubberneckers,
selfie malingerers, damn workers standing
around. Grateful or sure it wasn't an accident,
that it was not my accident, my unwashed
nine-year-old SUV laid out pathetically
under a septic tank trailer upturned
or a turkey-filled flatbed flinging feathers
everywhere.

Yes, I am sorry I would say, tried to get here
on time, I was just finishing my Thank You
notes, busy, and hacking out a last line of verse,
or two, or three, delayed while noodling out
the need for punctuation
and the exact place to spot

the unwilling but inevitable enjambment
to make the most of my
better late than never
end-stop.

The Long Shadows

Late in the day and you can notice
the long black shade cast
across the landscape.
Stones of all sizes and shapes rising,
becoming small mountain ranges,
the tranquil rosebush a wiry giant
tree, branches and thorns at jagged
angles to the low hill,
the dust-brown mound.
On the cross-hatched gray pathways
silhouettes guard like phantom
steeple chase hurdles, turning
the fence's sturdy pickets of wrought iron
into the imitation of bars.

At dusk there brews a thick light,
quieter, slower paced, painting color
onto a drab canvas, the muddy palette
merging lost details into blending
backgrounds, soon to be
only what the memory thinks
it sees, thinks it saw just a short
while not so long ago. Because
the blazing sun, less distinct,
goes down quickly
and though the long shadows stretch
so far, when the light is gone
they will never reach into tomorrow.

Goodbye Forever

Earliest memory,
the sweet-air scent of grass
and flowers,
warm sunlight on freckles.
Small fingers grasp
the large index finger.
Mother and toddler
descend the dirt road,
ruts and gravel.
Part way down,
a birch tree.
Snap a couple of twigs.
Taste it, chew it, don't swallow,
it's like Birch beer.
At the bottom a little stream,
round rocks in a foot of water
glisten, tadpoles wiggle about.
Throw your stick in,
let your explorer go.
The brook is piped under the road.
Hurry to the other side,
the sound of rushing water.
Watch for it.
It seems like a long time,
but it is moving quicker
than expected,
and there it is
popped out
the end
and already flowing away,
on white foam and bubbles.
Did you see it?
The child waving
bye-bye forever.

 **Tony Fusco** earned a Master's Degree in Creative Writing from Southern Connecticut State University and is Co-President of the Connecticut Poetry Society. He served as editor of *Caduceus*, the anthology of the Yale Medical Group Art Place, from 2002–2012, and is also a past editor of *Connecticut River Review, Long River Run, The Southern News, High Tide,* and *Sounds and Waves of West Haven.* His work has appeared in many publications including *Connecticut Review, Louisiana Literature, Red Rock Review, The South Carolina Review, Lips,* and *Paterson Literary Review.* His last book was *Java Scripture,* 2014, which is both serious and humorous, featuring poems about his youth, Savin Rock and Allingtown in West Haven, Connecticut. He is also the author of *Droplines* and *Jessie's Garden.* His poetry has won numerous prizes, including the prestigious Sunken Garden Poetry Prize. Tony has served as judge in numerous contests and competitions, has led many workshop classes and presentations at universities and high schools, and has presented at several conferences. He is owner of the publishing company Flying Horse Press.
http://flyinghorsepress.com/index.html

311 Shingle Hill Road
West Haven, CT 06516

www.ingramcontent.com/pod-product-compliance
Lightning Source LLC
Chambersburg PA
CBHW060419050426
42449CB00009B/2031